I WILL

LEARNING TO FOLLOW THE
REVOLUTIONARY
WITH TWO SMALL WORDS

DAVID TROTTER

nurmal

resources to inspire a new normal

Published in the United States
by Nurmal Resources.

ISBN-13 978-1-935798-08-8
ISBN-10 1935798081

Printed in the United States of America

Design and layout by 8TRACKstudios
www.8TRACKstudios.com

For Rick Fry
who inspired me to
follow the Revolutionary
with my whole heart.

TABLE OF CONTENTS

Introduction
JUST A FLICKER

It was just after midnight on January 1, 1991, and I was kneeling on a convention center floor in Fort Worth, Texas. As 5,000 other high school students surrounded me, tears began to flow down my cheeks. I felt this overwhelming sense of the presence of God like never before. I felt like something was going to be different.

In those moments, I sensed God calling me to be part of something that would forever change my life.

When I showed up to this same youth event several days prior, I had enormous plans for my life. Over the course of three days, my plans seemed so pale in comparison to what I was now hearing. It wasn't a particular person telling me that my plans were wrong, worthless, or a waste of time. I could feel that something in my heart was changing. What used to be "just a flicker" was being stoked into something so much more.

> God seemed to nudge me with a question that night.
> "David, will you devote your entire life to Me?"

I couldn't help but respond with a simple "**I WILL…**"

Until that point in time, my plan to become a professional photographer felt like a great idea in light of my skills and experience. It was the natural progression for my life. With a knack for the camera, I was the yearbook and newspaper photo editor at my high school, and I had won multiple awards for my efforts. I worked part-time at the local newspaper in Northern California shooting weekly high school sporting events, and photography had become my passion.

But, something changed on the floor of that convention center.

I remember every step up to the front door of my home after we returned from our trip. I put down my bags and told my parents that I didn't think I was supposed to go back to Kentucky to get a degree in photojournalism. In the midst of my tears, I noticed the smiles on their faces.

They knew what God was up to…even before I did. They were sensing a change of direction…even before I was. They wholeheartedly agreed with what I was sensing, and I've never been able to see the world in the same way since.

> I'll never be able to see the beauty of this world as something I just take from. **I must give back.**

> I'll never be able to see the problems of this world as something I just endure. **I must make a difference.**

I decided that I would devote me best energy, time, and resources to making a positive impact in this world. That was over 20 years ago, and I'm more passionate and devoted to the One who ignited this revolution within my heart.

Please know that the words you're about to read flow from my heart and my life. I'm investing my life to ignite a movement of revolutionaries who love God, love their neighbor, and impact their world. Much of my life is spent dreaming about how to spread the beauty of His love into more and more hearts.

Consider the book you hold in your hands a collection of sparks from my life to yours. To stir up this fire within you, two interactive components are provided as kindling for you or your group at the end of each section.

DISCUSSION: Flash Point

"Flash point discussion" questions are meant to ignite something within you as you dialogue with people in your life. Don't just skip over the questions. Wrestle through them. Allow the questions to cause that spark to smolder in your heart.

TAKE ACTION: Catch the Spark

At the very end of each section, there is also an opportunity to take an action step called "Catch the Spark." This is where you have a chance to integrate what we've been discussing in a very intentional way...a chance to put it into action!

As you read about THE Revolutionary and how he has ignited my heart, my prayer is that your heart will be ignited as well. If you're willing to take these simple action steps, I promise that you'll start to see some revolutionary results.

My hope is that you will begin to embrace your identity as...
a revolutionary.

David Trotter
December 2012

IGNITING A TWO-WORD REVOLUTION

Rewind to 1985. I was living in Bowling Green, Kentucky - a place you've probably never heard of - home to the one and only Corvette manufacturing plant. Aren't you impressed?

By the time 6th grade rolled around, I had toured that stinkin' plant 5 or 6 times as a kid. Every year, we'd load up one of those big, yellow clunky school buses and take the 3 mile journey past the edge of town, past Bowling Green High School, beyond Greenwood Mall, and right near all the tobacco fields. Our little legs would scurry around the big machinery gawking at all the helmet-clad workers causing a commotion of bangs and sparks.

I remember the 6th grade trip more than the others because of the mere presence of Arnold Smalley. His name fits for sure. Without a doubt, he was the smallest kid in the class. Of course, I found myself at the other end of the torment spectrum as the tallest. He was teased as the munchkin, and I was taunted as the giant.

Arnold had bright red hair that always seemed to find its way into a tussled state. Dark-rimmed glasses drew even more attention to his pointy nose. And, he wore the craziest outfits – an entire collection of dark-green sweaters, plaid pants, and black, leather shoes. For a kid of his age to wear black leather shoes to school, he was simply looking to get pummeled.

It was on the bus ride home from the Corvette plant in 1985 that little Arnold wove the most ludicrous statement into our lengthy discussion of superheroes. As we were debating the manufacturing process of Super Woman's invisible plane, he pipes up out of nowhere with, "Yeah…well…I'm a prince." I don't remember what country he indicated his royal heritage was derived from, but he clearly declared that he was a prince. We all roared with laughter, and poor Arnold slunk lower into the seat as we mocked him even more.

C'mon, a prince? Seriously? This is the kid that wraps his whole mouth around the metal protrusion on the school water fountain. This is the kid that wears black leather shoes to play kickball at PE. This is the kid that responds to every teacher's request for help by yelling, "**I WILL…I WILL!**"

I'm not sure what it was about Arnold that drove him to keep coming to school every day. He was mocked, tormented, and pummeled at every recess. Of course, I never laid a hand on the pipsqueak, but I witnessed plenty of others put a bruise on that red head of his. There was something about Arnold that was tenacious – something that kept driving him to keep going – something that motivated him to help others (even when everyone around him thought he was a big dork).

It wasn't his confidence or skills or even his royal heritage (if he even had one). It was his eagerness to make a difference. He didn't care what other people thought. Every chance he could get, he was ready to help someone out. He'd help teachers run errands around the school. He'd help new kids get their lunch. He'd even help his own bullies (without them strong-arming him) sharpen their pencils.

If there was even a hint of an opportunity to help someone, Arnold was all over it. He had this intense desire to be part of the action – to help out – to make a difference!

I don't know where Arnold is today, but my guess is that he's running a non-profit feeding the homeless and clothing the poor. Or, perhaps he's taking out all his pent-up aggression as a semi-pro wrestler in the Deep South. Or, maybe he truly is a prince, and we're the ones who are all idiots for not believing him.

Wherever Arnold finds himself today, I'm thankful for what I learned from him in retrospect. Arnold taught me two words that year that have re-surfaced in my mind recently. These are two simple words that have ignited every movement that has accomplished something significant. You may not realize the power of these two words, but you've seen them in action. You've heard them in the footsteps of the civil rights-era marches. You watched them in action as the Berlin Wall fell. You saw them in the protests of the students in Tiananmen Square.

You hear them unknowingly when someone chooses to respond to a need. It could be a small need that someone in your family has. It could be a need in your neighborhood, school, workplace, city, or even the entire world. At some point – if there is going to be a revolutionary change for the better (in any situation), someone has to take responsibility.

Someone must respond with, "**I WILL!**"

We live in a culture where we're tempted to pass the buck. We often resist taking responsibility for the problems that hinder our society from functioning at its best. Many of us are so busy dealing with our own 'to do' lists that we don't have room for much else. We just wish someone else would take care of it. Isn't that what our taxes go toward? Shouldn't our boss or the president take care of that? …Maybe not.

Maybe you're being called to be the revolutionary who takes action. Maybe you're the one who has been equipped by God to bring momentous change right in your world. Who said someone older, smarter, or richer should be the one to do it? Who said it has to be someone with lots of time on their hands? Why not you?

Revolutionaries Wanted

A revolutionary is one who brings about significant change in their area of influence. To say the least, our world is in need of passionate revolutionaries – not wimpy "go along with everything" people. You may not even be aware of this, but God has given every one of us an area to influence. God has given you a family, a neighborhood, and a school or a workplace. God has strategically positioned you to bring revolutionary change in that specific place at this unique time. Our world needs people who are willing to open their eyes to the needs around them and take responsibility. If not you, who? Who is going to help make this world a great place to live? Probably people like Arnold.

Can you imagine if hundreds of thousands of people started responding with "**I WILL**" when they encountered a need?

➔ When you see a co-worker who is struggling to get the job done, what if you said, "**I WILL**..."?

➔ When you see a neighbor who needs help with their dilapidated home, what if you said, "**I WILL**..."?

➔ When you see a litter-strewn empty lot that needs to be cleaned up, what if you said, "**I WILL**..."?

➔ When you see a person who needs food or shelfter, what if you said, "**I WILL**..."?

➔ When you see a village on TV in need of clean drinking water, what if you said, "**I WILL**..."?

➔ When you read about atrocities that are happening around the world, what if you said, "**I WILL**..."?

How would our world change if each of us were willing to take responsibility for the problems and needs around us? Don't you think we could change our culture? Frankly, I think we'd start a revolution.

Most of us think that problems in our culture are so big that we could never make a difference. That's crazy thinking! You've got to start somewhere. Besides, small changes lead to big changes, and big changes can lead to a revolution.

If everyone did his or her small part, we'd see a world that was characterized more by love than hate. Characterized more by education than ignorance. Characterized more by health than sickness. Characterized more by community than disconnection.

The type of revolution that I'm talking about was ignited some 2,000 years ago by a man named Jesus. Once the spark ignites in your heart, it burns hot with a passionate love for God and His creation - humankind. This isn't a lukewarm effort to be nice to people. Being nice to people has never changed the world. I'm talking about something that ignites within our hearts that just won't die out. It's like an all-consuming fire that compels us to take action – to spread His revolutionary movement of love around the world to each person we meet. And, the way you set yourself on fire with a passion to impact your world is by getting close to the sparks.

Over the next few chapters, we'll learn about five sparks that every revolutionary needs to encounter in order to be set on fire. Each spark will allow you to passionately respond with "**I WILL**" when opportunities to make a difference come your way.

Lame Excuses We Come Up With

I can hear some of you balking already. "Change the world? C'mon, be realistic. What can I really do?" We come up with all kinds of lame excuses that prevent us from taking action. Believe me - I've used every one of them on multiple occasions. When these excuses consume my mind, it's like the flicker within me gets flooded with discouragement. I'm not sure if I'm being fearful, lazy, irresponsible, or just incompetent, but here are a few that I struggle with sometimes. See if you relate.

1. I don't believe it's possible.
Yeah, that's what a lot of people say. Yet, other people have believed in the power of the "two-word revolution." Think about Martin Luther King. When few people would stand up for equality, what did he say? **I WILL**. Think about Mother Theresa. When few people were willing to help the neediest people in India, what did she say? **I WILL**. It is possible. It simply requires someone to respond.

2. I'm not _____ enough.
Fill in the blank. Smart, powerful, influential, rich, gifted. Whatever you think you are lacking is just an excuse. I don't want to

take anything away from Martin Luther King or Mother Theresa, but they're just like you and me. Ordinary people. The only difference is that they were willing to step up to the plate and say "**I WILL**", and they found people to join them who *did* have the resources that they were lacking.

3. I'm too busy.

Really? You're too busy to help other people? You're too busy to make the world a better place? Actually, you've never been too busy to do the things you really want to do.

Once you get a taste of the revolution, you won't be able to stop. You'll want to make a difference everywhere you go. There is nothing like seeing someone's life changed by your willingness to help.

For every need we come across, we can come up with an equally compelling excuse. Which one will we believe? The need or the excuse. I'm choosing to believe that the need is great, and I'm being called to change the world. Whether you know it or not – you are too!

My prayer is that the book you now hold in your hands won't just be my manifesto, but that it will become yours as well. This is my passion. This is what I've committed my life to. This is the type of life that I'm choosing to live. I have one life, and I just can't waste it. I can't waste it on "feel good" religion that is rooted in consumerism. I can't waste it on our culture's desire to have more and more stuff. I can't waste it on just taking it easy. I must respond.

Before you continue, I offer a word of warning. The words you are about to read aren't for the faint of heart. Be prepared to be challenged. Be prepared to be rubbed the wrong way. Be prepared to examine your life and ask some tough questions. If you take these words seriously, your life will be changed and so will the world around you.

I'm on a quest to change this world...for the better. Are you ready to join me? Are your bags packed with creativity and courage? Are you willing to learn new ways of thinking and responding? Are you ready to engage the world around you with a fresh perspective? You're invited to join me as we start a two-word revolution!

Say it with me now, "**I WILL!**"

DISCUSSION: Flash Point

1. Did you know someone like Arnold as you were growing up?

2. Who comes to mind when you hear the word revolutionary?

3. In your own words, how would you define a revolutionary?

4. Do you think it's possible to change the world for the better? Why or why not?

5. What lame excuses do you use that hold you back from making a difference in our world?

6. What's so powerful about these 2 simple words – "I WILL"?

FOLLOW THE REVOLUTIONARY

You've played follow the leader, right? You know the game. The one where somebody is chosen to get out in front, and everybody follows them around wherever they go. I loved playing that game at recess. As you can imagine, Arnold always wanted to be the leader. "**I WILL...I WILL**," he'd always yell.

Despite his exuberance, nobody wanted to follow him. You know why? Because he was scared to actually lead us somewhere that was adventurous. He'd just around in circles and the most courageous thing he would ever do is run down the steps, but it was always lame. He was willing to step up to lead, but he didn't really lead us anywhere other than wide-open spaces.

The best leaders were the ones who yelled "follow me" at the top of their lungs and took off running. You knew they were going to take you somewhere that was wild and dangerous – through narrow passageways requiring risk and courage and bravery. There was something inside you that just made you want to follow them – no matter where they dared to go!

You've got to know life is one giant game of "follow the leader." Catch this now. Life is one giant game of "follow the leader." Who you choose to follow in this life will determine the type of life you live on this earth and for all eternity.

There are thousands of organizations and companies yelling at the top of their lungs – "follow me." There are millions of people who want you to follow them down a road they believe is best for you. It's called the wide road – promising freedom and fulfillment!

Initially, it looks exciting, doesn't it?

I'll never forget the first time I went with my grandparents to Universal Studios. I was on vacation for the summer – out from Kentucky – and I was seeing incredible things for the first time. I was seeing a place where movies are shot – gaaawwwwlllly! I remember riding on a tour through the back lot and seeing this wide road with incredible homes on both sides. I thought to myself, "This is a cool street. I'd like to live here!" Then, we turned the corner down the next wide road, and we went behind all these homes. It was a façade. There was nothing there. It was just a shell – just the outside.

That's what many people have to offer when they say, "Follow me." They may not actually say to "follow me." But that's what they mean. When you're young and at a party and your friend says, "Everybody's doing it" – they're really saying, "Follow me." When you're feeling pressured by someone at work to do something you know isn't right – they're really saying, "Follow me." When advertisers are offering you stuff that you don't need and trying to help you mismanage your money – they're really saying, "Follow me."

The wide road is lined with vendors who are offering you all the things that look great on the surface – the pursuit of more money, more sex, and more power. Yet, it's just a façade. It looks great on the outside, but there is no depth – no substance. There's nothing to it – just momentary pleasure or excitement. Following this road won't lead to true fulfillment. Following people down this road will ultimately lead you to nowhere.

If life is one giant game of "follow the leader," there is one lone voice that stands out from the crowd. It is the voice of the One who created you. It is the voice of the One who is passionately in love with you. It is the voice of the One who seeks to lead you down the "narrow road." It is the voice of the greatest Revolutionary who ever walked the face of this earth. This Revolutionary knows what road is the most adventurous, the most fulfilling, and the one that will change your life. This Revolutionary knows what road will ignite something within you that will change this world.

This Revolutionary's name is Jesus.

If we're going to make a revolutionary impact in this world, we must begin by following the lead of THE Revolutionary.

Jesus Says, "Follow Me!"

As we read the ancient Scriptures in the Bible, they tell us that God designed a path – a road – for humankind to enjoy along the journey of life. Unfortunately, we came up with this crazy idea that we knew what was best for us. We thought we could blaze our own trail – find our own way – lead our own lives. The Bible tells us that in our effort to live this life apart from the leadership of God, we have all strayed off the path. We've all blown it!

The Bible calls all our screw-ups and mess-ups – sin.

Essentially, in our effort to find our own way, we've turned our back on God by walking away from Him and heading down the wide road. Can you imagine standing before the Creator of the universe, looking Him in eye, and saying, "Yeah, I know the best path for my life, and You don't. This is where You and I go our separate ways"…? It sounds ridiculous, doesn't it? That's because it is. Yet, this is exactly what we do through our words, attitudes, and actions

Yet, in His infinite love, God chose to come down on our level. Some 2000 years ago, God sent His Son to walk the face of this earth. He was and is the greatest Revolutionary of all time. He lived a perfect life and showed us a revolutionary new way to live.

Jesus came to lead us down the road that God originally intended for us to walk upon. He came to bring about significant change – not just in a "let's make the world a better place" kind of way. Jesus came as a Revolutionary to ignite a movement of love in the hearts of every human being.

He came to change the world!

Jesus triggered the first spark of this movement by calling 12 ordinary men to follow him…

"As Jesus was walking beside the Sea of Galilee, he saw two brothers, Simon called Peter and his brother Andrew. They were casting a net into the lake, for they were fishermen. "Come, follow me," Jesus said, "and I will make you fishers of men." At once they left their nets and followed him. Going on from there, he saw two other brothers, James son of Zebedee and his brother John. They were in a boat with their father Zebedee, preparing their nets. Jesus called them, and immediately they left the boat and their father and followed him." [1]

Two words that Jesus used over and over again to call his first followers – "**Follow me!**"

Despite their lack of formal training and inability to "get it" half the time, they were exactly who Jesus wanted. Jesus was choosing each one of them intentionally. Notice that Jesus changes the direction of their lives in this very moment. They were heading one direction as fishermen, but Jesus had something else in mind. He is calling them to be "fishers of men." He is challenging them to be part of the adventure of calling others to follow Him. Jesus is calling them to be part of the revolution.

I think one of the most amazing things about this account is what the men left behind. The Bible says, "At once they left their nets and followed him." James and John "immediately left the boat and their father." These guys recognized that everything around them paled in comparison to what Jesus was calling them to be part of. They recognized that Jesus was calling them to be part of a movement – something that would change their lives and the rest of the world forever.

As you may have heard, this movement of Jesus took a radical turn just three years in. It was at this point that Jesus was unjustly arrested. He was beaten, crucified, and killed. Jesus came to this earth not only to show us a new path, but also to pay the price for us turning our back on God in the first place. It is the through the death and resurrection of Jesus Christ – the greatest Revolutionary who ever lived – that we have the opportunity to choose a new path – the narrow road.

Before his death, Jesus challenged humankind...

> *"Enter through the narrow gate. For wide is the gate and broad is the road that leads to destruction, and many enter through it. But small is the gate and narrow the road that leads to life, and only a few find it."* [2]

This is Jesus' way of saying, "Don't just go along with the crowd down the wide road. Follow me down the narrow path. It leads to life – true everlasting life."

You Stand at a Crossroads!

Today you stand at a crossroads. If you look one direction, you'll see the masses heading down the wide road. You'll hear the voices of many who tell you...

> *"Everybody's doing it."*
> *"Nobody can tell you what to do."*
> *"If it feels good, just do it."*
> *"Just do whatever you want."*

If you look the other direction, you'll see Jesus heading down the narrow road. He's saying to you, "Follow me! Don't believe what you've heard from the masses. Yes, it will sound good, taste good, and feel good for a moment, but you'll waste your one and only life. Let me show you the way to true life. Let me show you the way to an amazing relationship with the One who created you. Let me show you how you can be part of a movement of love that's transforming the world."

Several years ago, two young men I knew personally died within a week of one another.

One was a friend named Joshua who was 23 years old, and the other was my neighbor named Hector who was 22. On July 19th, Joshua was driving down a hill in Yucca Valley, California, to get some food when his car veered off the road. He was ejected, and he died instantly at the scene. Seven days later on July 26th, Hector was riding his bike down the street from our home in order to pick up a pizza. A black Honda pulled up next to him, and a group of guys asked what gang he belonged to. Before he could answer, they shot him at point blank range. He died 2 blocks from his house...and mine.

Both guys loved their families, and they both loved life. But, there was one major difference between the two of them. They were on different roads. Hector was the wide road, and Joshua was on the narrow one.

Hector was known for screwing around – never finished high school, drank and smoked weed, and stole stuff around the neighborhood. Joshua was on a similar road, but on April 1st of the same year, he found himself at a crossroads. In that moment – on that night – Joshua heard the voice. He heard the voice of the One who was calling him down the narrow road. It was the voice of Jesus saying, "Follow me!"

It was on that night that Joshua chose to follow THE Revolutionary – not the masses. Joshua began to allow Jesus to turn his life around and revolutionize him from the inside out. Joshua moved to a new area to get a fresh start, and he started reading the ancient scriptures within the Bible every day.

Joshua and Hector were on two separate roads.

I want you to recognize that here's where the rubber meets the road. When you die and cross over into the next life, you can't change what road you're on. If you're on the wide road – heading <u>away</u> from God, you'll continue on the same road for all eternity. But, if you're on the narrow road – heading <u>toward</u> God as you follow Jesus, you'll spend all of eternity in the presence of your Creator.

You must realize that Joshua and Hector were following two different leaders!

Who Are You Following?
The question I have for you is simple. Who are you following? Are you following the voice of the masses down the wide road that leads to no-

where? Or, are you following the voice of THE Revolutionary down the narrow road that leads to life?

The Bible tells us that all we have to do is say "yes" to Jesus being the Master or Leader or Revolutionary of our lives...

> *"Say the welcoming word to God – "Jesus is my Master" – embracing, body and soul, God's work of doing in us what he did in raising Jesus from the dead. That's it. You're not "doing" anything; you're simply calling out to God, trusting him to do it for you. That's salvation. With your whole being you embrace God setting things right, and then you say it, right out loud: "God has set everything right between him and me!"* [3]

Once again - who are you following? Remember – you are at a crossroads. Look to your left. Look to your right. The great thing about life is that you can change direction at any point in time.

→ If you're running down the wide road with the masses...

→ If you've been running away from God your entire life...

→ If you chose to follow Jesus a long time ago, but you've veered off course...

→ If you've been avoiding a response to Jesus' call of "follow me"...

Now is the time to say "**I WILL**."

If that's you, maybe you would want to
take a step toward a fresh start in life...?

> *"Jesus, I want you to lead my life. I realize that I've been on the wide road that leads to nowhere. With your forgiveness and grace, I'm asking you to change the direction of my life. I'm now choosing to walk on the narrow road – following after you the best I know how right now."*

A decision to follow THE Revolutionary will change your life – not just right now, but for all of eternity. Essentially, you're joining a movement of revolutionaries who have been called by Jesus to live a life of love… loving God and loving His creation – humankind.

Or, maybe you're reading this thinking to yourself, "He's talking about somebody else. I'm already a Christian, and I've done that whole accept-Jesus-into-my-heart thing. I'm a good person, and I go to church when I can."

No – I'm talking to you, too. We're all at different places on our spiritual journey, but you're standing at a crossroads as well. You see there was a time when I called myself a Christian, but honestly – I wasn't following Jesus. It is possible, you know.

The term "Christian" has become nothing more than a label that's regularly hijacked by political parties, companies, pro athletes, rock stars, and a wide-range of religious nut jobs. It's become an adjective to describe cheesy tchotchkes and people who believe a certain set of doctrines – but often don't actually live out a revolutionary faith. Here's the truth - Christians go to church, but revolutionaries change the world!

I believe that Jesus is inviting us in a fresh way to join him in a revolution – a movement of love that's igniting around the globe.

> ➔ If you're tired of "feel good" religion rooted in consumerism…

> ➔ If you've been focused on what you can "get" rather than what you can "give"…

> ➔ If you've called yourself a Christian but haven't really been following after Jesus…

> ➔ If you've been playing it safe rather than listening to Jesus' call of "follow me"…

Now is the time to say "**I WILL**."

I'm sure you're thinking to yourself, "What does this mean for my life?" Frankly, I'm not sure. All I can tell you is that Jesus will lead you into narrow passageways that require risk and courage. If you embrace his call to be a revolutionary, you'll find yourself saying "**I WILL**" to things that you never dreamed were even possible.

Since I've been saying "**I WILL**" over the past few years of my life, Jesus has led me down a narrow road that I would have never chosen for myself. I've been stretched to do things, say things, and experience things that are far outside of the comfortable Christian culture I found myself in.

➜ I'm living in a neighborhood where I'm the minority.

➜ I've held parents in my arms as they've sobbed over the gang-related murder of their children.

➜ I've comforted an elderly gay neighbor over the death of her lifelong partner.

➜ I've befriended people who I would normally avoid out of fear by crossing the street.

➜ I've celebrated with village elders in southern India as I've dedicated numerous water wells.

None of this would have been my plan or my choice.

It's been a result of following Jesus down the "narrow road" and continually saying "**I WILL**" when he opens my eyes wide to the needs around me.

DISCUSSION: Flash Point

1. In your own words, how would you describe Jesus?

2. Have you ever heard the voice of Jesus calling you – not literally – but deep within your soul? If so, what was that like?

3. Who do you relate to more – Hector or Joshua?

4. Have you ever chosen to follow Jesus and join his revolutionary movement? If not, what's holding you back?

5. "Christians go to church, but revolutionaries change the world!" Do you think this is true? Why or why not?

6. Would you consider yourself a Christian, revolutionary, both, or neither? Why?

7. What scares you about fully turning your life over to Jesus and allowing him to be your leader?

TAKE ACTION: Catch the Spark

Grab a Bible, and turn to the book of Mark. This is a fast-paced, short account of the life, ministry, and death of Jesus.

Read it in one sitting. I know you've probably never read that much of the Bible all at once. Just do it. It won't kill you. It will only take a few minutes, and it's going to give you a fresh perspective on Jesus' life and words.

1. How do you see Jesus as THE Revolutionary?

2. What were you surprised by?

3. How do you see Jesus modeling the character and competence of a revolutionary leader?

4. Based on what you've read, are you willing to follow him wherever he leads you?

OPEN YOUR EYES WIDE

As a kid, I remember looking all over the house for a book or backpack or whatever. I'd be searching frantically to find it before I left for school, and I'd call upon the one whose eyes can see everything…Mom.

"Mom – where's my backpack?!?"
"It's on your bed. Have you tried opening your eyes?" she would respond – in only the way a loving mother can.

I hate it when someone has to go out of their way to show or tell me something that should be obvious to the average human being.

It's like all those times when I'm trying to find the "on" button…to whatever, and somebody walks up and just pushes it…as if it were obvious. I stand there thinking to myself, "Where did that come from? I didn't even see it."

Why are some things so obvious to one person, and yet another person can be totally oblivious? It's as if that backpack wasn't even present in my world. I could walk right by it and not even see it. Yet, someone else who has "eyes to see" can spot it right away. You've got to know that this isn't a new problem. It's been around for centuries.

Rewind about 2000 years to the time of Jesus.

Envision him hanging out with a motley crew of 12 guys who were at the heart of a new revolutionary movement. No matter what Jesus did, they had a horrendous time seeing what he wanted them to see. In frustration, Jesus asks them…

> *"Do you still not see or understand? Are your hearts hardened? Do you have eyes but fail to see, and ears but fail to hear?"* [4]

In other words, "Open your stinkin' eyes!" Even the guys who hung out with Jesus struggled with this.

Just because we possess a pair of eyes doesn't mean we actually use them. The truth is we become desensitized to things to the point that we're almost blind in everyday situations. Jesus knew that without open eyes, these 12 future revolutionaries would never be able to see the tremendous needs around them.

Listen to how he compares two groups of people in his day…

> "For this people's heart has become calloused; they hardly hear with their ears, and they have closed their eyes. Otherwise they might see with their eyes, hear with their ears, understand with their hearts and turn, and I would heal them. But blessed are your eyes because they see, and your ears because they hear." [5]

I don't know about you, but I can't see clearly all the time.

My eyes may be open, but sometimes I can't really see what's going on. Oftentimes, I will only see what I want to see. Ask my wife. She'll tell you how I'm blind to a sink full of dishes or a pile of dirty laundry on the floor. There's a lot of stuff in this world I close my eyes to, and sometimes I don't even realize my eyes are closed.

For instance, last week I was stressed out one afternoon, and I just took a quick walk around the block by my office. I couldn't believe all the stuff I had never seen before - even though it was right there in plain sight. I was surprised by how many types of flowers were planted next to our office. I had never even realized there was a volleyball court in our parking lot. And, I hadn't noticed some broken down walls, graffiti, and trash all over the place. Obviously, none of these discoveries are earth-shattering, but the fact is that I had never seen them before – even though I drive by it all multiple times a day.

Why? Because I'm usually driving at break-neck speeds zooming in and out of the parking lot to get into the office or head to an appointment. I'm unaware of what's going on around me in my immediate environment. In a sense, my eyes are closed. That's not only true about the physical objects around me, but it's true about the physical, emotional, and spiritual needs of people in my area of influence.

How about another example? When you drive up to a stop sign or freeway off ramp and a person who is homeless is begging, you don't make eye contact do you? No, you look ahead. You lock the doors, grip the wheel, and look at the car straight in front of you. Eye contact communicates recognition – which leads to interaction – which leads to relationship. Oftentimes, neither party wants relationship – one wants money, and the other wants to be left alone.

When you make eye contact with someone in need, it reveals your heart. Either you will feel something – like compassion – or it will reveal something else - like apathy or indifference or anxiety. You know that if you feel compassion, you'll need to take action. If you don't take action, you may feel guilty in some way. And, if you look them in the eye and feel cold, you feel guilty for feeling cold-hearted. So, we often come to the conclusion that it's better to avoid eye contact in the first place, and then we won't have to deal with any of those negative or troubling emotions at all.

Three Causes of Blindness

Maybe, just maybe, we're actually blind to the needs of the people and world around us, and we don't even know it or don't want to admit it. Sure, we physically see everything, but it doesn't register in our hearts somehow. Our eyes seem to have thin scales of "disregard" glazing over them to the point that we don't notice significant problems, challenges, and opportunities among us. We become blind when...

1. We're always in a hurry.

One of the biggest causes of blindness is speed. We just move too fast to see the needs around us. We cram our schedules so full that we're always in a hurry to move on to the next thing. In a culture that values efficiency and the use of time so highly, we're compelled to fill up every waking moment with activity and progress. And, if we do have the time, we may even feel guilty for not using it on something we deem as more worthwhile – on something that will help us get ahead in life.

2. We don't want to be inconvenienced.

Have you ever been walking in or out of a grocery store and had someone ask you to sign his or her petition? Have you just stared straight ahead and ignored them? You didn't want to be inconvenienced, did you? I've done it, too. The problem is that our desire for an easy life devoid of inconvenience causes us to stare straight ahead and ignore lots of problems in our world - and lots of people who are in need.

3. We know we'll need to respond.

This is the deepest and most intense cause of blindness. We know that if we truly allow our heart to see the need, we'll have to respond. We know our well of compassion will come gushing forth, and we won't be able to hold it back. We're in a "no win" situation in those moments. If we allow ourselves to see the need and don't respond, we feel horribly guilty. On the other hand, if we see the need, we may actually have to do something about it, and that may be equally as painful in our minds.

What causes you to go blind to the needs around you? What makes you want to avoid eye contact with someone who is struggling? What produces "disregard" in your soul?

Seeing Through God's Eyes

If we're going to be revolutionaries and bring about significant change in our areas of influence, we must first open our eyes wide. We need to see the world as God designed us to see it. We need to see the world around us in all its glory – the beauty, the pain, the tragedies, and the triumphs. We need to see it all – not just through our own eyes – but through the eyes of God.

What I often see as inconvenience, God see as an opportunity.
What I often see as painful, God sees as healing.

What I often see as risky and dangerous, God sees as transformational.

It's when we ask God to remove the scales of "disregard" and they finally fall off our eyes that we start to see things from a fresh perspective. It's in these moments that our eyes and heart seem to re-connect. What we now see fresh and anew creates a spark within us – allowing the compassion of God to ignite something powerful.

I love how Jesus saw the world through God's eyes. Jesus wasn't blinded by hurry, inconvenience, or the potential cost to him personally. He saw people right where they were – in the midst of their brokenness. In one such moment, it is written that…

> *"Jesus went through all the towns and villages, teaching in their synagogues, preaching the good news of the kingdom and healing every disease and sickness. When he saw the crowds, he had compassion on them, because they were harassed and helpless, like sheep without a shepherd. Then he said to his disciples, "The harvest is plentiful but the workers are few. Ask the Lord of the harvest, therefore, to send out workers into his harvest field."* [6]

Jesus didn't see the crowds and think to himself, "Oh man, this is going to take forever. Can someone just clear them out so we can get through?" No, Jesus sees beyond the surface and into their souls. He sees them as "harassed and helpless", and he has compassion on them.

It's no different 2,000 years later. The people around us are harassed and helpless in so many ways. We're harassed by companies to believe that we need more, bigger, and better – of whatever they're selling. We're harassed by the disconnection of community that's so prevalent in our culture. Many people are helpless to overcome a lack of purpose or meaning in their lives. Some are helpless to overcome addictions and relationship issues.

Jesus says, "Ask God to send more revolutionaries who will be compassionate toward these people."

When we truly see the world through God's eyes, we'll develop an intense compassion for humanity. Compassion moves beyond a momentary handout just to get someone to leave us alone. Compassion is a deep awareness of the suffering or needs of another coupled with the desire to relieve it. Without compassion for the people around us, we'll never be compelled to take action.

How Wide Open Are Your Eyes?

Several years ago, I was in the garment district of downtown Los Angeles purchasing a large amount of fabric for a project we were finishing at our church. After loading the thick roll of black material into the back of the car, I opened the driver-side door and started to place my foot in the vehicle. With my back turned, a tall, slender African-American man approached me from behind.

As I turned around, he said to me, "Excuse me, sir. I'm wondering if you can help me with some money to treat my foot problem. I'd like to sing you a gospel song, and if you like it, maybe you'll want to help me. You don't have to if you don't want to."

Frankly, I'm always a bit jumpy when I'm in the downtown area, and this time was no different. In preparation for my shopping trip, I grabbed several hundred dollars from my underwear drawer, because many of the garment district stores don't take credit card. Grabbing my saved-up Christmas money was much easier than heading to an ATM, and I was planning to simply get reimbursed for my expenses anyway. Well, it turned out that the store I went to did take credit card, so I was able to keep all the cash. My plan was to safely return it to its cozy underwear drawer at home in preparation for the purchase of a nifty gadget or new outfits or something else fun.

I don't know about you, but I'm not really excited about being approached by strange people in places I'm not familiar with – especially when I have a wad of cash in my pocket.

"This is not a good time to get robbed by a homeless guy," I thought to myself.

As he moved closer and closer to me, my back was pressed up against the inside of the open driver-side door. I had nowhere to go unless I rudely jumped in the car and sped away. Did I mention that I was driving the car owned by the church – plastered with the church's name and website all over it? Speeding away probably wouldn't be too cool…

After inspecting the filthy, infected wound on his foot, I found out his name was Monroe. I asked him where he was from and if he had sought help from certain agencies in the city. After sharing a bit of his life, I finally got around to asking Monroe about the song. He indicated that it was written about his mother's grief over his brother's gang-related death. After the heartfelt description, I reluctantly said, "Well, let's hear it."

Standing less than 3 feet away from me as my back pressed against the car door, he closed his bloodshot eyes, placed his calloused hands together, and starts to belt out the most amazing song. As he is singing at the top of his voice in the middle of the street, people are walking by us on the sidewalk gawking at this homeless, black man singing a song of lament right in the personal space of some jumpy, white guy.

I can imagine the stories people told their families at dinnertime. "You should have seen what I saw today!"

As Monroe poured his heart out about the loss of his brother, my heart was captured by the story that was coming through the song. My eyes started to well up, and I realized that I was having a spiritual moment on the side of the road in downtown LA as a homeless man was singing to me.

My eyes were open, and I was seeing through the eyes of God.

Ironically, Monroe's eyes were closed, and I started to ask God what I should do. It was like I instinctively opened my eyes wider toward Heaven looking for direction and guidance. Meanwhile, I knew that I had several hundred dollars in my pocket.

"Why couldn't I have had a measly $2 in my pocket?" I thought to myself. That would have made things so much easier. I could even see myself saying, "Here's all I've got – have a great day!"

As Monroe continued to sing, there was a message coming through my internal antennas – loud and clear. I sensed God was saying, "Give him $100."

"Really? No God, please, no!" I begged out in my head.
"Yep," God replied deep inside my gut.

As Monroe was finishing up the song, I stepped away to take a quick phone call. My eyes were open, and I had seen the need. I just had to respond. As I walked back toward Monroe, I rolled up the $100 and handed it to him. "Consider this a gift from God," I said.

Every considerate homeless person I've ever given money to has quietly walked away – slipping the money into his or her pocket. But not Monroe! He immediately unrolled it, and his eyes got huge.

Monroe yelled, "Oh my God!"

In a split-second, I had a smelly homeless man giving me a bear hug out in the middle of the street. His matted hair was pressing against my face, and he was gripping my lanky body with all his might. With tears in my eyes, I began to speak words of life and encouragement into his soul.

"Monroe, God will never leave you nor forsake you. Even in this dark hour, God has an amazing plan for your life. May you be guided by His voice and be filled with strength, wisdom, and creativity. May God protect you and bring all the resources you need to take your next step in life."

As he turned to walk away, he exclaimed, "I'm gonna go get something to eat!" I was overwhelmed, humbled, and convicted – all at the same time. I didn't need that hundred dollars. Frankly, I didn't need the other $200 that was left in my pocket.

What Can You Do?

As you dab your misty eyes, you may be thinking to yourself, "I can't give $100 to every homeless guy who comes up to me." You're right - you can't. But, just because you can't help every person doesn't mean you should close your eyes. Just because you feel overwhelmed by all the needs around you doesn't mean that you can go blind to the challenges and problems of our world.

The question is - what can you do?

It's so easy to get overwhelmed, isn't it? If we turn on the evening news, we're bombarded by problems all over the world. If we walk downtown in any sizeable city, we're aware of the plight of the homeless. If we walk through the halls at any high school, we'll hear and see things that engulf us with the needs of young people. If we're willing to jump on a plane and enter a culture that's foreign to us, we'll be confronted with the eyes of people who long for hope. If we'll spend time looking in our spouse's eyes as we talk about their day, we'll recognize their need for affirmation and encouragement. If we're willing to listen closely to our officemates, we'll hear all sorts of needs – from financial to relational to emotional.

You have a choice.

Will you close your eyes and act as if it's not there? Or, are you willing to say, "God, open my eyes even wider. Help me see what You see. Help me have compassion that ignites action."

You can do something.

You can do something that will bring about significant impact in your area of influence. You may not be able to change the entire world all at once, but you can change one life – today. When everyone else is turning his or her head to avoid the problem, may you stand strong and respond courageously with "**I WILL**."

DISCUSSION: Flash Point

1. Do you find it difficult to look needy people in the eyes? Why or why not?

2. Look back at the three causes of blindness. Which one do you resonate with the most? Is there something else that tends to blind you?

3. If Monroe had approached you, what would you have done? Why?

4. In what ways do you avoid seeing needs around you? In other words, how do you tend to keep your eyes closed?

TAKE ACTION: Catch the Spark

Go somewhere you wouldn't normally go and keep your eyes wide open. Maybe you need to take the train downtown or ride the bus across town. Maybe you need to walk down your street near those homes you avoid. Maybe you need to drive to the other side of city. Maybe you need to walk on the sidewalk, smell the atmosphere, and look into the eyes of the people.

1. What do you notice that you haven't noticed before?

2. How do you think God views the atmosphere and the people different than you might?

3. Based on what you heard and saw, what were you feeling? What were you thinking?

Spark #3

LOVE LIKE NEVER BEFORE

A number of years ago, my wife and I were living in Orange County, California and looking to re-locate about 30 minutes away to Long Beach. If you live outside of southern California, you may hear 'Long Beach' and think, "How luxurious!" Well…not exactly.

In our process of moving, people would regularly respond to our verbal moving announcement with raised eyebrows and a surprised "ooohhh." They may not say what they were thinking, but they didn't have to. Their face communicated plenty. If you've never been to Long Beach, it is a wonderful city with thousands of amazing people, but it is a very different place than Orange County. It is said to be on the other side of the "Orange Curtain." Does that tell you something?

While Orange County is often seen as neat, clean, and new, Long Beach is a bit older, more urban, and diverse.

With multiple Long Beach communities to choose from, we began placing offers on houses in an area just north of Long Beach called Lakewood. We quickly found out that Lakewood has two parts that are often termed 'Lakewood' and 'East Lakewood.' Because of soaring home prices, we were quickly outbid on five homes within a couple of months. Before we knew it, we were out priced in our desired neighborhood, and we started looking in 'East Lakewood' – on the other side of the freeway.

East Lakewood is not the most desirable area surrounding Long Beach. It is closer to areas with higher crime. The surrounding schools and stores aren't quite as nice. There is more graffiti and abandoned shopping carts. But, that's where we found a house – a house we could afford. For eight adventurous years, we lived on Lemming Street in East Lakewood with people from a variety of ethnic backgrounds - Latino, Filipino, and African-American.

If you're unaware, we're rather white, and we kind of stuck out.
At least, it felt that way to me.

I had never been a minority...until we moved to Lakewood. I had never lived on a street where people have family members who live in the garage. I had never witnessed street vendors selling roasted corn walking down my street. I had never lived next door to people who look like thugs. I had never watched a neighbor get hauled off to jail. I had never attended the memorial service of a neighbor murdered by gang members.

When we first moved in, we made a serious effort to get to know all our neighbors. We baked them cookies and introduced ourselves. We partnered with another family and hosted a block party. We even intentionally lingered out front to have the chance to say "hello." I know it sounds a bit weird, but I also started waving...a lot. I figured that if I waved at people who looked different than me, maybe that would somehow bridge the gap. Our neighbors must have thought I was crazy always waving at them. "Hey look, there's that weird white guy waving at us again!"

I've never thought of myself as being prejudiced, but our move to East Lakewood caused me to re-evaluate how I think about and how I treat people that are different than me. I had to be honest with myself. I wasn't that comfortable trusting (or even talking with) people who looked, talked, and acted different than what I was used to. I had to admit that I was more willing to trust someone if they looked, dressed, and acted like me.

How about you?

Do you avoid particular areas of your city or neighborhood in order to stay away from people who are different? Have you insulated yourself from "certain people" in the name of safety? Have you surrounded yourself with friends and family members who simply make you comfortable and at ease? Is it possible that your prejudices toward others are preventing you from loving like never before?

There's a guy in the Bible named James who wrote a lot about this – particularly how destructive favoritism can be. James was actually a younger brother of Jesus, and he was extremely committed to Jesus' revolution of love.

Favoritism Is a Nasty Word
On the surface, favoritism doesn't sound like a nasty word, does it? We all have favorites, right? Favorite foods, favorite clothes, favorite music, and favorite everything. But, what happens if we have favorites when it comes to certain groups of people? James makes it clear that this is divisive and harmful to humanity and the world at large. Listen to what James says…

> *"My dear brothers and sisters, how can you claim to have faith in our glorious Lord Jesus Christ if you favor some people over others? For example, suppose someone comes into your meeting dressed in fancy clothes and expensive jewelry, and another comes in who is poor and dressed in dirty clothes. If you give special attention and a good seat to the rich person, but you say to the poor one, "You can stand over there, or else sit on the floor" - well, doesn't this discrimination show that your judgments are guided by evil motives?"* [7]

James gets right to the point; we know exactly what his concern is. As someone who is part of this new revolutionary movement – as a follower of Jesus – don't play favorites!

Let me break it down for you. Favoritism means to favor the interest of one person or group and subsequently neglect others who have equal value.

Favoritism is completely inconsistent with the revolutionary movement of Jesus. Why? Because God doesn't have favorites.

One of Jesus' original revolutionaries named Peter says it this way...

> *"It's God's own truth, nothing could be plainer: God plays no favorites! It makes no difference who you are or where you're from - if you want God and are ready to do as he says, the door is open."* [8]

For us, it might be like a guy rolls up in his Benz wearing a stylish Armani suit, and he's looking mighty fine. Then, another guy walks in with an untucked flannel shirt, front tooth missing, and the nicest mullet you've ever seen.

You say to the guy in the Armani – "Oh, come sit right up here in this comfy seat."

You say to mullet man – "Feel free to stand over there or sit on the floor – whatever..."

James nails us with the rhetorical question, *"Doesn't this discrimination show that your judgments are guided by evil motives?"*

Essentially, he is saying that when we play favorites – we're putting one person down and lifting another up. Not only was playing favorites an issue in his day, but it's still with us in the 21st century.

In a world where we put so much stock in appearance, style, and possessions, favoritism is a natural result. The 'haves' and the 'have nots' often mistrust one another...for different reasons. Ethnic groups frequently congregate in pockets of sameness. Political groups, religious groups, and interest groups naturally cling to one another for comfort.

There is nothing wrong with feeling more comfortable with people who are like us, but does that result in treating others differently? The more you surround yourself with people that are just like you, the more likely you are to distrust people that are different. And, when we distrust someone, we're destined to "protect ourselves" in ways that disconnect us from relationship.

Continually, the Bible speaks of God's great love, compassion, and mercy toward those who are poor and in need. James is not saying to dishonor the rich, but he is calling us to honor both the rich and the poor. When a follower of Jesus dishonors someone who is poor or hurting or helpless, we treat him or her the exact opposite way that God treats them.

James goes on to say...

> *"You do well when you complete the Royal Rule of the Scriptures: "Love others as you love yourself." But if you play up to these so-called important people, you go against the Rule and stand convicted by it."* [9]

The Royal Rule that James is speaking of is "royal" because it is the message delivered to us by Jesus – THE Revolutionary. It governs all other laws dealing with human relationships. To love is supreme. Love is the root of all other moral and ethical laws on this earth.

In fact, Jesus tells us how important love is...

> *"'Love the Lord your God with all your heart and with all your soul and with all your mind.' This is the first and greatest commandment. And the second is like it: 'Love your neighbor as yourself.'"* [10]

Jesus and his younger brother James are calling us to love our neighbors. Not just the people that live to our right and left – although that's a good place to start – but everyone! This "everyone" includes the people you know and don't know who you work with, shop with, eat with, go to school with, and live near. "Everyone" includes people of every race, every language group, every religion, every life stage, every socio-economic level, every educational background, and every sexual preference.

The love they are both describing cannot include favoritism. We can't pick and choose who we love. Another follower of Jesus named John says it this way...

> *"We love because he first loved us. If anyone says, "I love God," yet hates his brother, he is a liar. For anyone who does not love his brother, whom he has seen, cannot love God, whom he has not seen."* [11]

Love and favoritism are mutually exclusive, and there is no way they both can exist in the heart of a revolutionary.

Do You Really Love Your Neighbors?

One night (when we still lived on Lemming Street), I pulled into our driveway after attending a wedding, and I noticed two young guys sitting in the back of a truck about four doors down. As I grabbed my suit jacket out of the backseat, God opened my eyes wide and something inside me said, "Go talk to them." Frankly, I hate those internal nudges, because they usually require me to get outside my comfort zone. They usually require me to say "**I WILL.**"

This time was no different.

I drove by these two guys on multiple occasions. Both of them were twenty-something Mexican men with shaved heads, wore oversized white t-shirts, and drank beer in the front yard. Frankly, they made me nervous. I don't think they were gang members, but they definitely worked hard to look the part. And, when I waved, they didn't look real excited to wave back.

As I walked toward the front gate of my white picket fence, I had a choice to make – walk down the sidewalk and introduce myself... or head inside. Finally giving in to that internal nudge, I muttered "**I WILL...I WILL**" under my breath and made my way down the crack-filled sidewalk one step at a time. As I approached, they both looked toward me somewhat startled.

"What's up guys? My name is David - I live down the street."

Inside my head, I'm thinking how cheesy that just sounded, and I'm hoping they don't pummel me like a little kid on the playground.

"How's it goin' bro? Wanna beer?"

You've got to know I'm not much of a beer drinker. In fact, I've never even tasted the stuff – not because I have anything against it; I just think it smells disgusting. So, I awkwardly declined and received a blank stare that fills the atmosphere with a peculiar nervousness. I desperately grasped for any subject that might provide some traction in the conversation.

It turns out they've been friends for over 20 years having both grown up on the street. We talked about Jorge's new truck, both their jobs (one blue-collar and the other white-collar), and the neighborhood all three of us lived in. As the conversation progressed, both them started talking about what's truly important to them. We even talked about the multiple re-models in progress and how that was increasing home values. And, we talked about how one of them had recently gotten pulled over for no reason.

"I don't know why they pulled me over. I've never even been in trouble with the cops."

"Really?" I naively responded.

"Yeah, we don't even like to go out and party. Man, I stay home. I'm a family man. I just want to play with my kids and hang out with my family. I'm not out gang bangin'. Just cuz I dress like this doesn't mean I'm out doing that stuff."

Obviously, they had no clue that their meandering conversation was confronting me head-on with my own preconceived ideas of what they were truly like. As we wrapped up the conversation, I walked back down the sidewalk feeling like I had just gotten punched in the stomach – not by them, but by my own prejudice.

In a matter of moments, my mental picture of them had shifted from gang-bangers to family men. I felt ashamed and outed all at the same time.

In our lives, favoritism plays out at many levels. We judge people and treat them differently for multiple reasons – not just because they are rich or poor.

→ We treat people differently because of their race.

→ We treat people differently because of their political views.

→ We treat people differently because of their education – or lack thereof.

→ We treat people differently because of the clothes they wear, the car they drive, and the neighborhood in which they live.

This list could go on and on…

Don't Just Love the Outside

Imagine this for a moment. Envision two gift boxes sitting on a table in front of you. One box is wrapped in beautiful gold paper adorned with a red velvet bow – immaculately put together. The other box is tied together with twine, dirty and crushed on one side, and has an odd odor.

Pretend that I'm giving you the opportunity to choose one box. There is something inside of both of them. Which one would you choose? The beautifully wrapped package that looks perfect? Or, the soiled one that has been crushed?

Most of us would typically choose the pretty one – whatever is up to the standard we have set. We like things with beautiful packaging on the outside, don't we? We like people who look nice, smell nice, talk nice, drive nice, live nice, and have nice amounts of money.

But, James is telling us to - "Love what's on the inside - not just the packaging."

Over the past several years, major shifts have taken place in my life. Now, over half of my friends are of a different ethnicity. Now, I have friends who have their PhDs and some who haven't graduated high school. Now, I hang with people who are millionaires and people that are barely making it. Now, I am close to people who have never had a speeding ticket and people who have spent significant time in prison.

Once you learn to love the inside, it ignites something powerful within you. You're not locked into this box that only allows you to associate with certain groups of people. You have the ability to move freely between socio-economic groups, educational levels, and stages of life. You have the ability to bring a message of love and hope to everyone – no matter where they are in life.

In our culture, we talk about loving the inside, but that's only if the inside looks nice. I'm not even talking about what people are like on the inside. I'm talking about the 'inside' that God created. I'm talking about that special stuff inside every human being. It's what differentiates us from everything else that God created.

Do you know that in God's eyes, every single person is inherently valuable? There's something on the inside of every person that needs to be honored, protected, and cherished. You know why? Because God created human beings (you and me) in His image! The very fact that God created someone means they are special – every single person – even the people that are different than you.

Beyond Mere Emotion to Action

This word "love" gets tossed around all over the place, and it's usually describing an emotion – something we feel. We talk about falling in and out of love. We talk about love at first sight. We talk about love as if it's something that happens to us rather than something we choose. The type of love that Jesus modeled is a love that goes beyond mere emotion to action. It's a love that knows no limits and has no boundaries. It's a love that will go to any length in order to meet a need, heal a wound, or offer forgiveness.

Obviously, you and I have been loved and have loved others in return. But, I want to challenge to you love like never before. It's easy to love people when we expect them to love us back. It's easy to love people when they look, act, sound, and think like us. It's easy to love people that love what we love. But, it can be challenge to love without strings attached.

Love is at the core of this "two word revolution" we're talking about.

It's the spark of love that enables you to say "**I WILL**" when no one else is willing to. What would it look like to put love into action right now in your neighborhood? Maybe you should begin by actually meeting your neighbors. Maybe you should take the time to get to know them. I know this might sound crazy, but what if you actually asked a neighbor over for dinner?

Honestly - before moving onto Lemming Street, I wasn't too concerned about getting to know my neighbors, but THE Revolutionary caused something to spark within me. This spark was a spark of love that has ignited a passion for my neighbors - wherever I live. Frankly, I think Lemming Street changed me more than I changed it.

What would it look like for you to love like never before? For my family, we're listening to Jesus as he nudges us to join him at work in his movement of love. Each time he says "follow me" – we do our best to say "**I WILL**." It's amazing what we found ourselves doing when we were willing to utter those two small words...

> → Attending the Spanish memorial service for our neighbor Hector where we were the only Anglos present.

> → Raising money from our neighbors to help pay for Hector's burial.

> → Inviting the 6 surrounding streets to our home for a 3-week marriage group led by a friend.

> → Baking and delivering cookies to the family with 6 kids that just moved into the 2-bedroom house across the street.

➡ Feeding the pets and getting the mail for a couple down the street.

If we are going to really make our world a better place, it will begin with how we think about and treat one another. Changing the world starts with a deep love for every single person God has created. It's hard to bring about significant impact when we we're busy favoring and dis-favoring certain people. Yet, when we embrace the rich and poor, tired and energetic, pretty and not so pretty, educated and uneducated – people will be flooding to join the movement to bring hope and health to this entire world.

Look beyond the outside package, and start to see the precious life that God has placed within each person. So, what's your next step? How are you going to get started?

Jesus' movement of love is a movement of action.

Love isn't something that we simply fall in and out of. It's something we choose to express as an act of the will. By taking action, you're joining Jesus in what he's already doing in the people around you. He's already loving them, and he's asking you to join him in spreading his love.

THE Revolutionary who started this "two word revolution" is calling you...to love like never before.

What's your response?
Are you ready to say, "**I WILL**..."?

DISCUSSION: Flash Point

1. Do you avoid particular areas of your city or neighborhood in order to stay away from people who are different?

2. Have you used the excuse of "safety" as a reason to avoid these people or places?

3. Have you ever felt pre-judged or discriminated against? What was that like?

4. How are love and favoritism unable to co-exist?

5. What type or group of people do you feel most comfortable being with?

6. How does your preference for this group cause you to dis-favor other people?

TAKE ACTION: Catch the Spark

Make a list of all the possible ways you can love your neighbors like never before. Go ahead – do it now! After you make your list, pick two things and do them this week.

Spark #4

IMPACT A BIG WORLD WITH A BIG VISION

Have your parents told you the same stories over and over again? My parents do…all the time. I don't necessarily fault them for it, because all parents do this sort of thing. You know what I'm talking about. You'll be hanging out with one of your parents, and a familiar scenario will present itself. Their mind is triggered by some random moment, and the story train starts to roll. There's no stopping it once it gets started. You just have to let them coast to the end.

The best thing about it is that they tell the same stories with the same intensity, excitement, and laughter every single time. And, as their loving child, I dutifully listen and nod my head in agreement – laughing at the appropriate times just like I did the very first time I heard the story.

One of those stories that my Mom tells over and over originally occurred when I was two years old. If you haven't been around two year olds much, they are just starting to communicate pretty well during this stage of life. They've moved beyond grunts and moans to a few syllables, and they can actually understand Mom and Dad as well.

As the story goes, my Mom and Dad were continually having difficulties communicating with me. I'd have my back turned to them, and they'd ask me to get up to take a bath or get dressed or pick up my toys or whatever. And, according to my Mom, I wouldn't even respond. I wouldn't turn my head. I wouldn't get up. I wouldn't make a move.

My parents became so concerned that they took me to the doctor to make sure I wasn't going deaf. As my Mom recounts the day, the doctor took me into a room and performed a routine hearing test. Can you imagine my Mom standing outside the examination room as her only child is being tested for hearing loss? Can you imagine the emotions welling up as she waited on the edge of her seat to see if something was wrong with me?

After a few minutes of close examination, the doctor comes out giggling to himself, and says, "Your son can hear perfectly fine…He's just ignoring you!"

My Mom shifted from that concerned, compassionate parent to the enraged Mom from you know where.

Many of us are tempted to treat Jesus in a similar way. We're so busy doing our own thing that we often ignore his quiet voice up ahead saying, "Follow me." Sure, we may hear what he's saying, but we're so busy, distracted, or disinterested that we don't respond with the passionate "**I WILL**" that He's looking for. We may even act like we don't hear Him and choose not to respond.

One of the first steps to making a difference in your world is not only keeping your eyes wide open but your ears as well. We must continue listening for direction. Whether you realize it or not, there are hundreds of ways to make a positive impact in your family, neighborhood, school, workplace, and city. What are you specifically being called to do? You've got to listen to find out.

Being a Christian Isn't Revolutionary

I don't know if you've looked around recently, but we live in a really big world. With over 6 billion people living in almost 200 countries on 7 continents, there are an endless number of opportunities to bring about significant impact for the health and well being of the humankind. Not only does Jesus call us to make an impact on the micro level by helping individual people that surround us. But, there are enormous opportunities to make a serious impact on the macro level. Think about all the life-giving, revolutionary changes that can be made in the areas of education, healthcare, housing, public policy, sports, the arts, and entertainment – all in the name of the One who ignited this revolution of love.

Why do we shirk this opportunity (or even responsibility) onto other people? "Well, I guess people in power will make all the decisions about what we watch, how we live, and what goes on all around us." Really? Are you sure? If you have a passion for something, why not seek to transform your neighborhood, your workplace, your industry, your city, or even the entire world – within the context of your passion?

Unfortunately, we tend to limit our faith to what's experienced during 1 to 2 hours on Sunday morning and maybe a mid-week Bible study group of some sort. Yet, Jesus is calling us to be revolutionaries who allow his teachings and leadership to permeate our entire lives. For many of us, being a Christian is the farthest thing from being revolutionary. It means that we go to church. It means that we're nice to people. It means that if we're really committed we may give God some of our money, read a book called the Holy Bible, and talk to Him when we need something.

There has to be more. There's got to be more to following Jesus than that. Why would Jesus say all the revolutionary stuff that he said if he just wanted us to boil it all down to something that was palatable? I don't think so. Frankly, I think Jesus has to be really bummed. I think Jesus is pretty disappointed when we create a fun show on Sunday to learn about him and sing happy-clappy songs about his death, but we're totally ignorant about the things that are destroying our world.

We're more informed and concerned about who got voted off the latest reality show than we are about human trafficking. We're more informed and concerned about the newest fashion trend in jeans than we are about the AIDS pandemic in India. We're more informed and concerned about the hip new drink at Starbucks than we are about the water shortage in villages throughout Africa.

Why? Because it doesn't directly affect us. "If I don't have to deal with it on a daily basis, then it's not my problem." We may not actually say that, but that's how we live. What's directly in front of us gets most of our attention.

In his 1958 book entitled "Stride Towards Freedom," Martin Luther King states...

> *"Any religion that professes to be concerned with the souls of men and is not concerned with the slums that damn them, the economic conditions that strangle them, and the social conditions that cripple them is a dry-as-dust religion."*

Jesus never intended to create some dry-as-dust religion that was celebrated once a week. He was igniting a movement of revolutionaries who genuinely loved him, one another, and the world around them. He came to this earth proclaiming a message of sacrifice on behalf of others. He modeled the message of sacrifice through his death on our behalf, and he calls us to follow in his footsteps. Jesus says...

> *"If anyone would come after me, he must deny himself and take up his cross and follow me. For whoever wants to save his life will lose it, but whoever loses his life for me and for the gospel will save it. What good is it for a man to gain the whole world, yet forfeit his soul?"* [12]

What good is it to live your one and only life for your own benefit? What good is it to spend 70 maybe 80 or even 90 years walking this earth just to live for the weekends?

There's got to be more.
The "more" is found in saying "**I WILL**" when Jesus calls us to sacrifice.

The revolutionary life that Jesus is calling us toward is one of denying our own immediate gratification for the benefit of the men and women around the world in need of his love and hope. Taking up our cross means that we're willing to suffer a bit for the good of others. It means that we're willing to sacrifice physically, financially, emotionally, and maybe even relationally. When we suffer a bit, it may feel like we're losing our lives, but in reality – we're finding what true life is all about. Christianity isn't revolutionary, but following Jesus is.

Finding Life on the Other Side of the World

In 1998, I met a revolutionary named Suresh Kumar. He was visiting southern California all the way from southern India in order to share how the movement of Jesus was impacting remote villages on the other side of the world. Through his thick accent and in between chewing this foreign substance known as a fish taco, Suresh shared with me and a couple of friends about the intense need for clean water, health care, and basic education among the Dalit caste – otherwise known as "untouchables."

The church where I was on staff was considering a partnership with Harvest India – the organization that Suresh's mother started over 40 years ago. Frankly, I wasn't interested. I sat there eating my tacos listening to a guy talk about the problems that disease-infested water causes when it's used to wash the animals and drink for dinner – all at the same time. I'm thinking to myself, "These people need to wise up. What are they thinking? Somebody should help them get a clue."

Somebody should help…but not me.

I have never been interested in learning about global humanitarian work, listening to missionaries, giving to missions, and especially going on a mission. I was not interested on multiple levels. First of all, it always sounded dirty, and I like to be clean. It sounded hot and sweaty, and I like to be cool. You name it – I wasn't interested in it. Foreign languages, weird food, funky clothes, dirty kids, and potential diseases. No thanks!

But on a deeper level, I knew there was another reason why I wasn't interested in what he was talking about. The bottom line is - I couldn't handle seeing the need. I know myself. I have a tough exterior that looks confident and together, but I fall apart when I see people in pain or suffering. I start to get all choked up and teary-eyed, and I feel guilty about my indifference.

When I see a need, I feel compelled to respond. In reality, I HAVE to respond. So, if I don't want to respond, I avoid seeing the need. I just don't want to have to deal with it.

Fast-forward 5 years to 2003. I got a call from a friend who thought it would be good for Suresh and I to hook up again. I was thinking to myself, "Great, I've got to look at more pictures of people who are suffering. This should nice." Meanwhile, Jesus is up ahead on the narrow road yelling back at me…"Follow me!"

Within months, I found myself boarding a plane with 3 friends to fly around the other side of the world. After multiple planes, layovers, trains, and buses, we ended our 56-hour door-to-door adventure. Count them…56 hours of travel. Little did we know, this was just the beginning.

My eyes were open wide as we careened down a narrow road dodging cars, auto rickshaws, bikes, trucks, buses, people, goats, cows, water buffalo, and pigs - all tossed together like some sort of chaotic Indian soup.

I quickly discovered that the movement of Jesus was vibrant and pulsing on the other side of the world – perhaps even more than in the US. In some ways, it was like stepping back in time 1,000 years as we walked through remote villages. Absolutely everything was handmade except for an occasional bike and water well. Although there is nothing inherently wrong with living at such a primitive level, many of these people didn't even have basic food, water, or medical care. The degree of sickness and disease was profound.

Beyond physical needs, the spiritual needs were overwhelming. We saw hundreds of Hindu temples set aside to worship over 1 million gods. I stood amazed as people worshipped trees, animals, and stone objects. My heart was heavy as I saw thousands of people deeply searching for truth, hope, and joy. One night at an open-air meeting, I found myself standing in front of 20,000 people sharing about the revolutionary love of Jesus, and I finally saw the need. Their eyes and ears were wide open

– ready to receive this new life. And, my eyes and ears were finally wide open to hear Jesus whisper.

It was on that first trip to India that Jesus whispered in my ear, "A big world needs a big vision."

For those two weeks, my mind was stretched every time I heard Suresh share the big vision that God gave him for his nation. With over 1,500 village churches, 25 or so orphanages, multiple elderly homes, a nursing school, and several Bible colleges, Harvest India is only getting started.

How can one man have such a big vision from God and yet others of us don't have any vision at all? Is it because God only gives a "big vision" to certain people? Or, is it because only certain people are listening?

As I got off the plane at LAX, I kept having this thought run through my head, "I have seen the need, and I MUST respond." All those years of avoiding what I didn't want to see had been wasted. I was trying to save my life, but I was actually losing it. Now that I was willing to lose my life, I was finding it. Ironically, I was finding life on the other side of the world.

Mahatma Gandhi was once asked by a reporter, "What is your message?" He responded, "My life is my message."

I'm realizing how true that statement really is. I can say anything I want, but when I live it, it truly becomes my message. Words are cheap in our day and age, but actions speak loudly.

In the last 8 years, I've been to this great nation 8 times, and I recently produced a documentary on 25 orphans living along the railway in southern India (www.motherindiafilm.com). The sacrifice of time, energy, money, and comfort pale in comparison to the impact that I can make in the lives of people who Jesus loves and died for.

These people in need aren't just living on the other side of the world in India – they're everywhere. Every country in the world – including wherever you live – is filled with people in need and people who are suffering. They may not be physically suffering like so many people in India, but they're suffering in other ways. Are you willing to allow God to take your mind, heart, and maybe even your physical body outside of your local context? Are you listening to the big vision that he is calling you to be part of?

Are You Listening for Your Big Vision?

I believe that God doesn't just give big visions to certain people. I believe He has a big vision for every person's life – including yours. The question is, "Are you willing to listen?"

I'm talking about a vision that's so big that there's no way that you could see it come to fruition on your own. It's so big that you'll need other revolutionaries to help you and THE Revolutionary to do all that stuff that would be impossible for you to do in the natural.

> ➔ *Why wouldn't Jesus be willing to use you to change the world?*

> ➔ *Why wouldn't Jesus be able to empower you with strength and courage?*

> ➔ *Why wouldn't Jesus be excited to invite you to join him in bringing hope and healing to a hurting world?*

There's absolutely no reason! All you have to say is "**I WILL**."

It's that simple. When you're finally willing to release your right to a comfortable, convenient, self-satisfying life, that's the moment that Jesus will start to give you a big vision.

It's in that moment that whatever you see that's missing or wrong with the world becomes a spark that ignites something within your heart. Before you are willing to lay down your life and your rights, whatever seems missing just causes you grief. It causes you pain and torment, because it just bugs you. But now, whatever is wrong with the world becomes the fuel that engulfs your life with passion to bring about transformation. There's something within you that wants to set things right.

So, what's missing or wrong in your world? When you lay your head down on the pillow at night, what grips your heart with angst? When you watch TV at night, what images cause your heart to pound faster and faster? When you read the newspaper, look through a magazine, or drive through your neighborhood, what ideas flood your mind?

Is it the educational system in your city? Or the plight of the homeless? Or the orphans who live on the streets around the world? Or the sex trade that swallows up the lives of the young? Or the family down the street who is going through a bitter divorce? Or the trash-strewn lot that nobody seems to care about?

Unfortunately, if we are able to open our eyes wide enough to actually see the need, most of us have thick filters surrounding our brains that prevent us from taking action. We come up with a long list of excuses as to why we couldn't possibly do whatever it is Jesus is calling us to do.

Our challenge is to remove the filters from our minds that prevent us from embracing the big vision – to remove the filters that say…

✗ "Normal people don't do things like that."

✗ "I need to stay in my stable job for the sake of my children."

✗ "That might be dangerous or risky."

✗ "Moving there would be unrealistic."

✗ "People would think I'm crazy."

✗ "I don't think that would actually work."

Get rid of those filters. Those are the thoughts of the masses heading down the wide road. Revolutionaries are willing to remove all impediments that are holding them back from fully yielding their life to the One who ignited the movement in their heart to begin with.

What's the big vision that Jesus has been whispering in your ears? Have you said "**I WILL**" yet?

DISCUSSION: Flash Point

1. Why do you think we tend to limit our faith to a couple of hours on Sunday?

2. Would you say you're more informed about pop culture or current world problems and challenges? Why?

3. Jesus said, "If anyone would come after me, he must deny himself and take up his cross and follow me." What would that look like in your life right now?

4. When you see a need, what do you tend to do?

5. Do you feel like God has given you a "big vision" for your life? Why or why not?

6. If He has given you a "big vision", are you living it out? If not, what's preventing you from taking your next step?

7. What filters do you have in your mind that hold you back from doing something "big"?

TAKE ACTION: Catch the Spark

Begin to explore what God's "big vision" for your life is...

➔ Ask yourself, "What do I think is wrong or missing in this world?"

➔ Talk to God. Listen to what He says.

➔ Talk to a friend. Ask them what they see God doing within you.

➔ Research what you sense is "missing" in the world on the Internet.

➔ Make list of 10 things you can do to cultivate what you think is missing.

➔ Get off your butt and actually do 1 or 2 of them!

INFLAME THEIR HEARTS

Knock, knock, knock.

"May I help you?" the woman shouted in a thick accent through the security door.

"Hi, my name is David, and this is my wife Laura. We just moved onto Lemming, and we're here with some cookies to welcome ourselves to the neighborhood."

Okay, so I didn't quite say it that way, but that's essentially what we did. Since no one really made an effort to welcome us, we thought we'd take a crack at it. Within months of moving into our new home in East Lakewood, we baked a ton of cookies for our neighbors. (In reality, I just came up with the idea - my wife did the actual baking.) After the cookies cooled, she wrapped each plate beautifully with festive red cellophane and Christmas ribbon, and we set out with our 2 kids (a 4 year old and a 10 month old at the time) to walk the neighborhood.

Dodging a pack of Chihuahuas, several ice cream trucks, and a guy selling cheese out of a portable cooler door to door, we made our way up and down the street to meet our neighbors. Some people were excited to meet us and others were a bit chilly in their reception. The response that was universal was shock. People couldn't believe that we were coming around to introduce ourselves.

C'mon – who welcomes themselves into a neighborhood? The unwritten rule in most neighborhoods is to stay to yourself. Be cordial, wave politely, but don't expect much in terms of interaction. The problem is that revolutionaries don't buy into that type of independent, "stick-with-your-own-kind" mentality.

Revolutionaries know that God has called them to inflame the hearts of others. Loving the people around us and making a positive impact in our neighborhoods, workplaces, and schools is tremendous. But, if we're going to ignite a movement of revolutionaries, we must allow the fire that is burning within us to inflame the hearts of those around us.

Within the heart of every revolutionary, there is a fire that burns with passion…

→ For God and His plan to revolutionize the world with His love.

→ For Jesus and his willingness to die on our behalf.

→ For individuals who are in desperate physical, emotional, and spiritual need.

→ For people who are wandering through life on the wide road.

As my family and I walked up and down Lemming Street, that fire was burning within us. We wanted to inflame the hearts of people who we were just meeting. We wanted them to know about God's plan for their lives and how they too could be part of a revolutionary movement of Love. We weren't trying to shove anything down anyone's throat – just wanting to be a blessing. With that fire burning in our hearts, our desire was simply to connect and make ourselves available. Frankly, we had no clue what that simple act of love would produce in the days to come.

Spreading the Fire

A few months later, my wife got a knock at the door. It was a neighbor from down the street who remembered that I was a pastor, and her brother needed a letter of recommendation to become a godfather to his nephew in northern California. My wife was nice enough to give her my cell phone number so the neighbor's brother could call me. Within a couple of hours, a random guy named Richie called me asking for this letter that was being required by the priest.

"What exactly does the letter need to state?" I asked.

"Well, I guess it needs to say that I go to church and that I'm a good person and stuff," he replied.

At this point, I was thinking to myself, "Who in their right mind calls someone they don't even know to ask for a letter of recommendation?" But, I didn't think that question would get us anywhere, so I took another route.

"Okay...um, well, do you go to church?" I asked.

"Not recently, but I've been thinking about it," he said.

"Well, tell me about your relationship with God. Do you believe in God?"

"Oh yeah, I've been to church a few times, and I believe that He exists – but I've got a lot of questions,"

"Are you interested in going to church to learn a bit?"

"Sure, I guess..."

"Okay, here's my proposal. If you're willing to come to Revolution Church a couple of times and watch a DVD about the life of Jesus, I'll write a letter saying that you believe in God and are in the process of finding a church that's a good fit for you. If you don't like Revolution, you don't have to come back. Just give it a shot. How does that sound?"

"Sounds great."

I kept thinking, "I hope Jesus will be okay with a little bribery this one time."

Meanwhile, I was soothing my guilt with Richie's willingness to take a next step.

"So, when exactly do you need the letter?"

"Well, we're leaving in the morning at 5am…"

"So, you need it right now?" I asked again as I looked down at my watch which was displaying 9:05pm.

"Yeah, kind of…" he responded hesitantly.

I quickly typed up a short reference letter on letterhead, grabbed a DVD, and headed down the street to his home. I wasn't sure what would happen, but I kept saying "**I WILL**" each time Jesus nudged me to continue down the narrow road. To my surprise - within a couple of weeks, Richie brought his entire family to church on a Sunday morning, and they started connecting – with God and the people around them.

Meanwhile, Laura began to develop a friendship with a woman named Valerie who lived diagonally across the street – just loving her and praying for her marriage regularly. Although her husband and kids weren't interested in God, there was a flicker in her heart that was just waiting to be stoked. Despite her anxiety, she was willing to join Laura each Sunday at church to start learning about God and His plan for her life.

At the time, we were hosting a weekly group in our home to study the teachings of Jesus. Our neighbors would see people coming and going with kids in tow, and I'm sure they were wondering what was going on. We were hesitant to invite Valerie, Richie, and his wife Selina – thinking that it might be overwhelming for them. Well, Jesus was already at work – stoking the flicker in their hearts - nudging them to join us.

On a particular week when we had quite a few people out of town, all three of them asked if they could come to the group. After we got over our shock, we said, "Sure, we'd love to have you!"

As we worked our way through the curriculum, Valerie, Richie, and Selina began to ask questions that were leading us off-track…and I didn't appreciate it. I kept re-directing their questions back to the topic at hand until I finally realized what was happening. They were at a crossroads. All 3 of them had been following the masses down the wide road, and now they were starting to hear the voice of the One saying, "Follow me."

I closed my Bible and set aside my notes, and I began to answer their questions. I began to tell them about how God created them with a purpose. I explained how each of us chooses to turn our back on God and head down the wide road. I shared with them about Jesus and his sacrifice on our behalf – giving us the opportunity to experience God's grace. I told them about the fresh start that was available to them by responding to Jesus' call to join the movement.

All they had to say was "**I WILL**."

I began to see tears running down Valerie's cheeks as I shared this good news with her. Then, I looked to my left and saw Selina's eyes welling up with emotion as well. Richie seemed pensive and a bit overwhelmed.

I asked a simple question, "Is there anyone who would like to begin to follow Jesus tonight?"

Valerie said, "Yeah, I do."

Selina chimed in, "Me too."

And as Richie began to tear up as well, he said, "Yeah, that's what I need too."

"Jesus, I want you to lead my life. I realize that I've been on the wide road that leads to nowhere. With your forgiveness and grace, I'm asking you to change the direction of my life. I'm now choosing to walk on the narrow road – following after you the best I know how right now."

I couldn't believe it. Several months prior, Laura and I were walking down Lemming Street with a fire in our hearts – wanting to invite people to join us on this adventure of following Jesus. We didn't know what to say or even how to say it. Cookies – that's all we could think of. Months later, I was sitting in my living room in awe as Jesus was calling out to three people who were choosing to follow Him for the first time.

He was whispering, "Follow me."
They whispered back, "**I WILL**."

I helped them talk to Jesus that night and tell him that they wanted to get off the wide road and start walking on the narrow one. On that night, Valerie, Richie, and Selina joined the revolutionary movement of Jesus. They joined a movement of millions of people who have surrendered their lives over the past 2,000 years to the One who is the greatest Revolutionary of all time. They became part of the "two-word revolution" that has absolutely transformed their lives.

- ➔ Lives that were characterized by anxiety are now transformed by peace.
- ➔ Lives that were desperate for meaning are now flooded with purpose.
- ➔ Lives that were filled with chaotic relationships are now marked by intimate passion.

The flame that was burning in our hearts was now burning in theirs. That night was the beginning of a personal revolution for each one of them… and for me.

Who Will Tell Them?

That night I realized that God not only has a plan to use me to bring his love to people in practical ways, but He wants to use me to tell people about this personal revolution that they can experience firsthand. I'll never forget walking out my front door that night and looking up and down the street. I kept asking myself, "Who will tell them? Who will have the guts, the fire, and the passion to tell them about THE Revolutionary?"

A guy named Paul, one of the fieriest followers of Jesus to ever live, asks questions that kept me awake that night...

> *"Everyone who calls, 'Help, God!' gets help." But how can people call for help if they don't know who to trust? And how can they know who to trust if they haven't heard of the One who can be trusted? And how can they hear if nobody tells them? And how is anyone going to tell them, unless someone is sent to do it?"* [13]

These are the questions that stoke the fire in the heart of a revolutionary. If you found yourself answering each one with a passionate "**I WILL**," your heart has been captured. Once you've allowed Jesus to ignite your heart with his love, there's something inside of you that's compelled to invite others to join you on the adventure of following him.

You start to see people in a different way.

You start to see them as precious men, women, boys, and girls that God uniquely created and longs to guide down the narrow road. You start to see how people have been lulled into a "wide road" lifestyle, and you simply want them to experience the type of life that you've started to experience.

Frankly, once you help someone join the movement of Jesus, you're ruined. You'll never be content with just being a nice Christian who goes to church and assumes that everyone will find his or her way through life. You're ruined, because now you know how high the stakes are. You're ruined, because now you know how Jesus can totally transform someone's life. You're ruined, because now you won't be satisfied with what other people call normal.

You want to be part of a revolution.

Safe and Dangerous
If your heart isn't pumping with passion right now, may I suggest that you look inward? Perhaps a craving for comfort or contentment has become the force that sedates your heart. Let me be clear...

Comfort has never catalyzed a movement.
Contentment has never ignited a revolution.

No great movement that has impacted thousands of lives or brought about significant change has ever been generated out of the heart of someone who was focused on comfort.

To be a revolutionary requires that you leave behind comfort to boldly and passionately follow Jesus on the adventure of spreading his love – inflaming the hearts of the people around you.

To be a revolutionary – one who brings about significant change in your area of influence – you most not be lulled into contentment. Contentment has never brought about significant change.

If we are content with what we have and what we're experiencing, there will be no fire burning within us that is needed to inflame the hearts of our friends and family. Comfort and contentment are not the elements needed to ignite a revolution.

The elements that I'm finding to be absolutely necessary in my life – if I'm going to impact my world – are safety and danger. These two ingredients seem to be diametrically opposed to one another, but in fact – they function hand in hand.

Safety *fosters a sense of security.*
Danger *creates an atmosphere of possibility.*

Without safety, there is no sense of security – no sense of acceptance, love, or encouragement. Without danger, there is no atmosphere of possibility. Without danger, there is no possibility of transformation.

The most beautiful picture of a person who is "safe and dangerous" is Jesus. During his entire ministry on this earth and even today – Jesus integrates safety and danger in a way that is absolutely revolutionary.

Jesus is SAFE.
He chose to meet us right where we are – human beings on planet Earth. He has our best interests in mind – to give us a full life. He welcomes everyone into relationship with Him – everyone.

But, Jesus is also DANGEROUS.
He calls us to follow him with our entire lives – leaving everything behind. He teaches us a whole new way of life – different from how we used to live. He empowers us to live a revolutionary lifestyle – trusting him at every turn.

What would it look like to live a "safe and dangerous" life? What would it look like to meet people right where they are? And, at the same time, have this fire burning within us that will inflame their hearts?

Revolutionaries are SAFE when...

➔ They're honest and transparent about their own difficulties in life.

➔ They don't assume that people know anything about Jesus.

➔ They love people right where they are – no matter what their lifestyle is all about.

➔ They help people in need with no strings attached.

➔ They cross racial, socio-economic, gender, educational, and political barriers.

➔ They willingly take the role of a servant in a relationship.

Revolutionaries are DANGEROUS when...

➔ They're clear about how Jesus has impacted their thoughts, attitude, and behavior.

➔ They can talk about Jesus in ways that are informative and personal.

➔ They challenge people to think about what life's really all about.

➔ They live out their values even when it's not easy or popular.

➜ They make decisions that cause other people to think about their own life.

➜ They say things that are challenging and thought provoking, but not self-righteous.

It's the combination of the safety and danger in the life of a revolutionary that provides the spark that ignites someone else's heart. If you're just safe, there's no possibility of inflaming their heart. If you're just dangerous, you may end up burning them in the process.

I know it's starting to get harder, but keep going. Don't stop. It can start to feel overwhelming when it's not just about loving people with our actions – now God is actually calling us to use our words. Movements are launched with actions, but they're fueled with words. God wants to use the words within you to invite people to start following him for the first time. Paul – that fiery follower of Jesus – reminds us of this…

> *"God put the world square with himself through the Messiah, giving the world a fresh start by offering forgiveness of sins. God has given us the task of telling everyone what he is doing. We're Christ's representatives. God uses us to persuade men and women to drop their differences and enter into God's work of making things right between them."* [14]

Do you really want your friends, family, co-workers, and neighbors to be stuck with masses on the wide road of life for all of eternity – disconnected from God? Wouldn't you rather have them walking next to you on the narrow road – passionately following in step with THE Revolutionary? If so, are you willing to go to any length to have them join you? Are you willing to get outside your zone of comfort and contentment to inflame their hearts?

I don't know about you, but…"**I WILL.**"

DISCUSSION: Flash Point

1. How many neighbors on your street or in your complex do you know?

2. Do you regularly seek to engage in conversation to build ongoing relationships? Why or why not?

3. Paul asks the question, "And how can they know who to trust if they haven't heard of the One who can be trusted?" What is your response to his question?

4. Have you ever helped someone follow Jesus and join his revolutionary movement? If so, what was it like?

5. How does comfort and contentment hold you back from inviting others to join you in following Jesus?

6. Do you feel more safe or more dangerous? Why?

TAKE ACTION: Catch the Spark

Draw a simple hand with five fingers in the space below, write the names of five people who are not followers of Jesus. Begin to take some action steps toward inflaming their heart...

➜ Pray for them to be blessed each day this week.

➜ Ask them if there is anything you can pray for.

➜ Share with them a way that God has impacted you in the last month.

➜ Be open to sharing with them about the adventure of following Jesus.

SET YOURSELF ON FIRE

As an adult, I now look back on the claims of Arnold Smalley in 6th grade, and I start to smirk. What kid actually thinks he could convince his pre-pubescent peers that he was a prince in a far-off land? Did he dream of changing our opinion of him? Did he envision a rise in his playground popularity? Did he really think we would say, "Wow, Arnold, you're soooo cool!"?

None of those things ever happened. Actually, the opposite effect took place. We ridiculed and mocked him with ever-increasing levels of intensity. From his quirky, green clothes to his incessant sniffles to his constant tripping over those unlaced, black leather shoes. I use the word "we" loosely. I don't remember actually mocking him out loud, but my head was definitely filled with an abundance of ridicule. C'mon...wrapping your mouth around that protruding part of the water fountain is absolutely disgusting!

If it were really true that Arnold was a prince, why was he attending elementary school in Bowling Green, Kentucky? Why did he have all those crazy clothes? Why was he such a twerp?

In our 6th grade minds, a prince was tall and strong. Yet, Arnold was short and scrawny. To us, a prince wore elaborate outfits with a crown on his head. We never saw Arnold wear a crown, and his hair was always a mess. We thought a prince should have a nice car or chariot or something like that. But, Arnold's Mom dropped him off every morning in a beat-down Buick.

What kind of prince is that?

If Arnold could have pulled off such a claim, it would have been the biggest prank of our 6th grade year. But, we never bought it – not even more a minute. Here's why…

Arnold lacked convincing evidence.

There was nothing about the way he looked, talked, smelled, or behaved that led us to believe he had an ounce of royal blood in his body. In our minds, he was the antithesis of royalty. Even though Arnold was ingenious in his desire to help everyone around him, he was lacking in evidence to prove his outrageous claims.

Have you ever noticed how often people try to be something they're not? For some reason, human beings feel the need to claim to be all sorts of things. From lying on a resume to dropping names to over-selling credentials to changing our personality based on the scenario. We paint ourselves in a certain light so that people will accept us. We act differently in particular situations in order to get ahead in life. We allege to be someone else so that we'll feel better about ourselves.

We can change the way people perceive us by the way we present ourselves in both words and actions. If what we present to the people around us resonates with who we truly are, there is evidence that our claims are true. If we are inauthentic, the lack of evidence in our lives will be a resounding gong that drives people away from us.

Not only is this true in relationships and in the workplace, but it is also true when it comes to our faith.

Have you ever known someone who presented themselves as spiritual or religious but they lacked evidence in their lives? Have you ever met someone who said they were a Christian but you'd never know it by the way they treated the people around them? All of us have.

If we have a true faith, there will be substantial evidence that THE Revolutionary is actually revolutionizing our lives. If our faith is burning with intensity, people will be able to feel it radiating from within us. They'll feel the sparks coming near them. They'll see a fire blazing that stands out from the dim-lit lives of wide-road walkers.

Evidence of a Fire Is Needed

James – Jesus' younger brother – says that "good deeds" are the evidence we're looking for. Without good deeds, there is very little evidence that our faith is still burning. He goes so far to say that our faith is dead – the fire has burned out – without evidence to the contrary. James writes...

> *"Dear brothers and sisters, what's the use of saying you have faith if you don't prove it by your actions? That kind of faith can't save anyone. Suppose you see a brother or sister who needs food or clothing, and you say, "Well, good-bye and God bless you; stay warm and eat well" - but then you don't give that person any food or clothing. What good does that do? So you see, it isn't enough just to have faith. Faith that doesn't show itself by good deeds is no faith at all - it is dead and useless. Now someone may argue, "Some people have faith; others have good deeds." I say, "I can't see your faith if you don't have good deeds, but I will show you my faith through my good deeds."* [15]

By definition, faith is a belief, trust, and loyalty to a person or thing. James is writing a letter to followers of Jesus – people who have put their faith in the One who has invited them into this revolution. So, James is asking them, "What good is it if a person claims to place their faith in Jesus, but has no actions to back up this faith? Can it save them?"

James presents the question and goes on to "suppose." Suppose someone is in need, and we say, "Oh, I'm so sorry. I'll pray for you. Good luck!" – but we don't do anything to help them. Suppose one of your friends needs help moving. Suppose your family is in need of a listening ear. Suppose a co-worker is overwhelmed with a project. Suppose your neighbor is unable to repair his or her home. Suppose a friend needs help paying this month's rent. Suppose you see the aftermath of a natural disaster overseas. Suppose you see people who are experiencing a great injustice – locally or globally.

Will you say, "**I WILL**…"?
Or, will you turn your head and walk the other way?

James asks, "What good is that kind of faith?" Talk is cheap, but actions speak louder than words. If faith is not accompanied by action, your faith is dead. The fire is out cold. You have no faith at all.

Whatever it is that you're claiming to have, it's not a living, life-changing, motivating, faith in Jesus if your life doesn't have the evidence of action. To paraphrase James, "Faith plus nothing equals…nothing." Faith without good deeds is no faith at all.

If you walked into a courtroom and were asked to present a case outlining your faith, would you have enough evidence? What type of evidence would you bring? Would you open up your briefcase and pull out documentation that you go to church? Would you somehow bring evidence that you talk to God? Maybe, you'd bring certification that you believe the right things. All those things are good and well meaning, but this isn't the evidence that James is looking for. Nor is it the evidence that the people around you are watching for.

People Want to Watch

Have you ever been watching the evening news as they report on a fire? I'm always in awe of the sophisticated trucks and equipment spewing out water all over the place, and it's incredible to watch the heroic efforts of the firefighters knocking down walls to save victims and rescue pets. But, in a weird way, I'm drawn to the edges of the scene. I think it's intriguing how many people just show up to stand and watch.

During my senior year of college, my wife and I lived on campus in a small apartment. One night, we abruptly woke up to loud sirens and flashing lights right outside our 2nd floor window. I jumped out of bed and opened the blinds to see a raging inferno across the parking lot. The college theatre was going up in flames!

Do you think I crawled back in bed and said, "Oh, it's no big deal honey. A building is just on fire. Good night..." No, I threw on a pair of shorts, grabbed my camera, and got as close as I could. I wanted to see what was going on. I wanted to be part of the action. I wanted to say I was there to see it all.

There's something about fire that just makes us want to watch. We're drawn to the light, the heat, the sparks, and the intensity. We're in awe of its power, and we want to see what's going to happen next. It's no different with your life.

When your life is on fire with a passion for THE Revolutionary...

When your love is red hot with intensity for humankind...

When your faith is burning brightly with a lifestyle of good deeds...

When your focus is on igniting a movement of revolutionaries...

People want to watch.

An 18th century revolutionary known as John Wesley once said...

"Set yourself on fire and people will come for miles just to watch you burn."

When people see evidence of a fire within you, they'll begin to talk. Word will spread that there's something to see. Much like the scene of a roaring blaze, they will show up to stand and watch.

They'll be drawn to your faith, your passion, your sacrifice, and your commitment to impacting your world.

Striking the Match

The key to being a revolutionary – one who brings about significant change in your area of influence – is to set yourself on fire. Rather than give you a formula for action, let me ask you a few questions as a way to strike a match upon your life...

1. How close are you to THE Revolutionary?

THE Revolutionary is already at work – revolutionizing the world. Jesus is healing hearts, restoring hope, spreading love, and saving lives. He is leading the way down the narrow road, and he's calling out to you and me..."Follow me."

It's his life that burns the brightest. It's his heart that is on fire with a passion for humankind. It's his lead that we must follow. The closer you get to him – the brighter your fire will burn. Are you aware of what he's doing? Are you listening to him? Are you following his instructions? Are you staying on his heels?

Take a moment and reflect on how you'd like to stay closer to THE Revolutionary. What would that practically look like?

2. How do you need to start thinking differently?

Living a revolutionary life requires that we get rid of the wide-road filters that envelope our mind – filters that say, "Normal people don't do things like that" or "People would think I'm crazy." In fact, in the ancient Scriptures of the Bible, we're told not to conform to the thinking of this world. "Be a non-conformist" – we're told. Paul writes…

> *"Do not conform any longer to the pattern of this world, but be transformed by the renewing of your mind."* [16]

In other words, allow Jesus to revolutionize the way you think. How have you been thinking about life, faith, people, and this world in a way that doesn't align with the thinking of THE Revolutionary? If you're not sure, ask him. He'll begin to reveal things that you didn't even realize about your thinking. He'll show you how it's holding you back from being the revolutionary that he's called you to be. And, he'll show you how a different way of thinking will fuel the fire of the revolution in your heart.

As you've been reading, how do you sense that your thinking needs to change? How will you seek to allow Jesus to revolutionize your thinking?

3. What do you need to leave behind?

On every great adventure, you always have to make choices in terms of what you'll take and what you'll leave behind. There are so many things that we hold on to in this world that function as needless dead weight. They prevent us from fully embracing our role as a revolutionary in this global movement.

At one point in his life, Jesus comes across a rich young man who is quite proud of his life. The man asks, "What must I do to inherit eternal life?" Jesus promptly sets him up by reminding him of the 10 Commandments. In his pious way, the man tells Jesus that he's kept them all since the time he was a little boy. Jesus knew this couldn't possibly be true, so he hones in on the real focus of this man's life. The Bible says...

> *"Jesus looked at him and loved him. "One thing you lack," he said. "Go, sell everything you have and give to the poor, and you will have treasure in heaven. Then come, follow me." [17]*

It's not that his money and physical possessions were bad, but they were holding him back. He needed to leave them behind in order to be fully freed up to follow THE Revolutionary. What do you need to leave behind? Physical possessions? Prejudice? Anger? Resentment? Greed? Fear? An Addiction? What is it?

What's weighing you down right now from following Jesus with total abandon down the narrow road? What's holding you back from being a revolutionary and making a significant impact in your area of influence?

4. What do you need to start doing – right now?

I've found that if God is stirring up something deep in my heart, I need to take action as soon as possible. If I don't respond with an immediate "**I WILL**", most likely I'll miss what He's trying to tell me in the madness of my daily life. Jesus said...

> *"The kingdom of heaven has been forcefully advancing, and forceful men lay hold of it."* [18]

In other words, this revolutionary movement started by Jesus some 2,000 years ago is advancing no matter what. It is a movement of love that is passionate, dynamic, and forceful. And, those who are part of this movement are forcefully spreading it – not through violence or anger – but through an action-oriented life. Revolutionaries don't sit around waiting for someone else to meet the need or make the change. When revolutionaries see the need, they MUST respond.

What's wrong or missing in your world? Based on the needs you see and the big vision that God is giving you, what do you need to start doing – right now?

Manifesto of a Revolutionary

Don't believe the excuses that seek to douse the fire in your heart. Now is the time. You have one and only life, and you just can't waste it. Don't waste it on "feel good" Christianity that is rooted in consumerism. Don't waste it on our culture's desire to have more and more stuff. Don't waste it on just taking it easy. You must respond. THE Revolutionary is ready to change the world through you!

I'm on a quest to change this world...for the better. Are you ready to join me? Are your bags packed with creativity and courage? Are you ready to think and respond in new ways? Are you ready to engage the world around you with a fresh perspective? Join me as we start a two-word revolution!

I am a revolutionary. I will not be satisfied with life as normal, and I will not listen to the voice of the masses. I'm listening to the lone voice of THE Revolutionary calling me down the narrow road. I am sacrificing comfort and contentment in order to love like never before. I am part of a movement of the heart that is changing the world – one life at a time.

Who will speak up for those who have no voice? Who will step up when someone is in need? Who will stand up in the face of injustice? Who will show up when no one else will?

I WILL.

I WILL

ENDNOTES

[1] Matthew 4:18-22 [NIV]

[2] Matthew 7:13-14 [NIV]

[3] Romans 10:9-10 [MSG]

[4] Mark 8:17-18 [NIV]

[5] Matthew 13:15-16 [NIV]

[6] Matthew 9:35-38 [NIV]

[7] James 2:1-4 [NLT]

[8] Acts 10:34-35 [MSG]

[9] James 2:8-9 [MSG]

[10] Matthew 22:37-40 [NIV]

[11] 1 John 4:19-20 [NIV]

[12] Mark 8:34-36 [NIV]

[13] Romans 10:13-15 [MSG]

[14] 2 Corinthians 5:18-20 [MSG]

[15] James 2:14-18 [NLT]

[16] Romans 12:2 [NIV]

[17] Mark 10:21 [NIV]

[18] Matthew 11:12 [NIV]

For more resources by David Trotter:
www.davidtrotter.tv

www.ingramcontent.com/pod-product-compliance
Lightning Source LLC
Chambersburg PA
CBHW021134020426
42331CB00005B/770